Since You've Been Gone...

J.L. Foster

ISBN 979-8-89428-836-9 (paperback)
ISBN 979-8-89243-335-8 (hardcover)
ISBN 979-8-89243-336-5 (digital)

Copyright © 2024 by J.L. Foster

All rights reserved. No part of this publication may be reproduced, distributed, or transmitted in any form or by any means, including photocopying, recording, or other electronic or mechanical methods without the prior written permission of the publisher. For permission requests, solicit the publisher via the address below.

Christian Faith Publishing
832 Park Avenue
Meadville, PA 16335
www.christianfaithpublishing.com

Printed in the United States of America

To my wife, Stephanie—
You are my best friend, my soulmate, and more than I
could have ever hoped to find in a partner for this life.
Thank you for being my better half and the
glue that holds our family together.
I love you…even if everything.

To my kids: Brooke, Reese, Madelyn, and William—
You are each so perfect in your own
way and I love you all so much.
Thank you for giving me the best family I could ever ask for.

To my mom, Marilyn—
I could never tell you how thankful and proud I am of you
for all that you have been through and done for me.
Thank you for raising me to be a man of God and showing me
every day how to live your life with a selfless, loving heart.
I love you.

To my readers—
I hope in some small way this book helps ease your heart and
brings you happiness in remembering the person special to you.
Remember…it's never goodbye; it's until you're together again.

Dear Daddy,

　　Since you've been gone, things haven't been the same. I've grown up so much, and so much has changed. You wouldn't believe the places I've seen and things I've done, but I wish you were here because they would all be more fun. I'm writing this letter so that you can know all the things that I've learned and ways I have grown. So when you read this letter, I hope that you smile because I miss you so much and we haven't talked in a while.

Since you've been gone, I've explored new things, like the day at the beach with our family last spring. I'll be honest with you, I didn't want to go. It was cloudy and dreary, and I felt lonely and cold. But as we arrived, all the clouds disappeared. I walked down to the water...without you, it felt weird. I sat in the sand and dug for a while, just like we used to do, and it made my heart smile. Before too long, I had the most amazing sand castle, until the water rushed in and I watched it unravel. As the waves washed away my best castle ever, I remembered you saying, "Treasure each moment... Nothing lasts forever."

Since you've been gone, I've tried something new. I got a new dress and some tights and some shoes. I tried so hard to learn my routine. I wanted it to be perfect because kids can be mean. When the day finally came for me to perform, it was almost my turn, I felt shaky and warm. They called my name to go out on the stage. I felt my legs freeze like I was stuck in a cage. "What if I mess up? What if I fall? What if I panic and forget it all?"

I thought back to our memories of all the things we had done. I could still hear your words, "It doesn't have to be perfect… Go out and have fun." I stepped out on stage and could feel you there, as I danced and twirled my dress through the air. When I finished, I stopped and took a bow. I wish you could've seen me, you would've been so proud!

Since you've been gone, I've tried to be strong. Some days go fast, but some feel long. When everything's done at the end of the day, I miss talking with you...it's just not the same. Our family feels different like we're missing a piece. It feels like forever since you tucked me to sleep. But we talk about you and all the things we miss. The one I miss most is your hug and kiss.

I want you to know I've practiced my prayers. I know that they're working because I can feel you there. I remember your words and the way you smile. I wish you could hold me for just a little while. Even though I miss you, I know one thing. You'd want me to be happy and to dance and sing. I guess what I'm really trying to say, is I'm trying to be happy and remember you each day. I know it will never be the same as before, but I can feel you with me and I'm not sad anymore. So I hope when you read this you smile and know you're always with me wherever I go.

Love,
Me

Dear Sweetheart,

   Since I've been gone, things haven't been the same. I'm in heaven now and so much has changed. I want you to know that not a day goes by that I don't miss you and wish I was by your side. But God is here and He talked with me. He showed me His plans and what will come to be. He made me promise not to say, but I can tell you one thing...it will be worth the wait. In the meantime, I hope you enjoy the ride and remember He's working in you one day at a time.

Since I've been gone, I've watched you grow. I've seen every day, all the highs and the lows. I was there with you that day at the beach when you felt like your heart was missing a piece. I brushed away the clouds and let the sun shine down. I watched you light up and wash away your frown. And the day that you danced all alone on stage, I was there by your side helping you to be brave. I stood and watched as you lit up the room and wished you could feel how much I love you. So whatever life brings, remember you're not alone and that you're so much stronger than you'll ever know.

Since I've been gone, I've missed your hugs and all the smiles and laughs and things that I love. And although we can't talk or hug each day, just remember I'm here every step of the way. I'm with you on days you don't feel like your best and when no one understands the hurt or the stress. I'm with you on days you feel worried and scared, when you feel all alone and think nobody cares. I hope on those days that you talk to me, whether it's praying for help or whatever you need. I can promise you one thing that will always be true, I hear every word and I'm never far from you.

I hope you remember how amazing you are, and I hope that you always follow your heart. Remember that God has a special story for you. It might not be easy, but He will help you through. And I promise I'll be there every single day and that I'll leave little signs along the way. So don't be scared when you stumble or fall because you have an angel in heaven with you through it all.

The very last thing that I want to say, is that you make me proud every single day. And I hope you take chances and reach for the sky, because I know in my heart you were meant to fly. Never lose faith, stay strong, and you'll see. He's growing you into who you're meant to be.

So I hope when you read this, you smile and know I'm always with you wherever you go. And always remember I'll love you 'til the end, and that it's never goodbye...it's until we're together again.

Love,
Me

About the Author

Hey friends! I'm Jeff, and I was born and raised near Omaha, Nebraska. I graduated from the University of Nebraska at Lincoln with a bachelor's degree in psychology and from the University of Nebraska Medical Center with a doctorate in physical therapy. Currently, I work as a physical therapist at a nonprofit, faith-based organization, helping people recover from a variety of different conditions every day. I truly love doing what I do and am so grateful to be able to share the talents God gave me with my patients each day.

Now for the best part, my family! I'm married to my best friend, Stephanie, and together we have four amazing kids. Brooke: my incredibly beautiful and talented daughter who amazes me with her kindness every day. She is an avid reader and can never have too many books on her shelf. Reese: my son who reminds me every day how to have a servant's heart and love others as God intended. He is incredibly thoughtful and loves beating me in Nintendo. Madelyn: my daughter and never-ending ball of creativity. Whether it's writing, dancing, or putting on a play, she puts her heart and soul into everything she takes on and makes us proud every day. William: my son and firecracker of our family. He is always there to help you smile, and no one is better at getting a laugh than this kid.

You guys are my everything and I'm so proud of you all. Thank you for always supporting me, encouraging me, and being the best family I could ever ask for.

Printed in the USA
CPSIA information can be obtained
at www.ICGtesting.com
LVHW070917021124
795334LV00003B/72